Some Far Horizon

Some Far Horizon

Poems

Francis Minay

Covenanters Press

Covenanters Press
an imprint of
Zeticula Ltd,
Unit 13,
196 Rose Street,
Edinburgh,
EH2 4AT,
Scotland.

http://www.covenanters.co.uk
admin@covenanters.co.uk

First published 2023
Text Copyright © Francis Minay 2023
Cover photograph:
Longniddry Beach, Sunset. © Francis Minay 2023

ISBN 978-1-905022-42-7

To the Memory of My Parents
William & Phyllis Minay
my Sister Priscilla
and to the parents of my wife,
John & Kay Burns
and all departed loves

- each loss of each image
is single and full, a thing unrequited,
plighted in presence to no recompense -

The Prayers of the Pope – Charles Williams
from
The Region of the Summer Stars

Acknowledgements

This second book of verse is the result of much
encouragement from family and friends, old and new,
many of them appreciative recipients of my first book
A Summoning Half Sensed.

I would like once again to record my indebtedness
to my wife's cousin Alan MacGillivray
for his expert eye in looking over
many of the poems gathered here,
and to my friend Dr. Chris Hanvey
for getting me going again
after a period in the doldrums.

I must also acknowledge the generosity of
Mrs. Chloe Teacher for giving her blessing
to the publication of the poem sequence
"Chagall at Tudeley"
which commemorates the sad and untimely loss
of her sister Sarah.

My wife continues to be a major support, nor must I
forget members of the congregation of St. Donan's
Church, Nostie, who inadvertently inspired the Christmas
poems in this book.

Contents

Foreword

The writer Charles Williams says somewhere that there is a widespread perception that "life is a good thing and somehow unbearable". And, not but. It is nevertheless a statement that invites-demands even!- qualification. No two people's experiences of life are the same, and those experiences differ as widely as the opportunities afforded them to make something of it. Those for whom life is or seems entirely unbearable are probably not the people who will be found reading poetry: yet it remains true that many of the most profound responses to the phenomenon of life in music, painting, poetry, sculpture, or any of the performing arts, emerge not only from experiences of the ineffable, but from precisely those situations in which life is experienced as most unbearable. Hope – the human spirit reaching out towards the as yet unattained, perhaps unattainable – is, I would like to think, what informs most, if not all of the verses in this book. Hence the Title – *Some Far Horizon*.

The seventy five poems contained in this book may readily be seen as reflective of the two opposing poles to which Charles Williams' statement bears witness. Here are celebrations of what is and what has been good, not only in my own life, but in the universal experience of people as a whole: the beauty and significance of the world, the universality of love, the joy of friendship, the wonderful quiddity of things, the capacity of great art to enrich and give meaning to human life. Added to these, are testimonies to my own not unquestioning approach to the Christian verities which have shaped my life for good. That is one pole.

The other is reflected in a significant number of poems that explore the universal experience of loss and grief. The sequence of seven poems *Chagall at Tudeley* is as much an exploration of grief as it is a celebration of the beauty and significance of the memorial glass to which the death of a daughter gave rise.

Then again, over a two year period – but particularly in its first stages – the Covid 19 Pandemic devastated families and communities in a way perhaps unprecedented since the Second World War, and finds expression here in a further seven poems that reflect my own personal response to the unfolding tragedy. Added to these more identifiable woes is that sense of a malaise in contemporary society that undermines the human capacity for joy and creativity, the mental anxiety to which one contemporary answer is the attempt to reconnect with Nature. These opposites are reflected in the poems *Under a Dark Sky* and *Forest Murmurings.*

However, celebration is never far from my attempts to give to the most intense human experiences some sort of form, and the three final poems in the volume, each of which arises out of a different remembered experience, and each of which possesses a different valedictory quality, are all celebrations of life as essentially gift.

Some Far Horizon

Portentous Idyll [1]

Thick cloud in a portentous pall lies low
above the Law,
but seawards, out across the Firth of Forth,
the last of evening's light
dropping beneath the curtain's close confinement,
gilds the hills of Fife,
firing the far horizon in a sea of flame,
flooding the nearer land with strong long-shadowed rays.

No breath of wind
stirs the sparse grass upon the dunes,
the sluggish waves
not hastened or delayed in their slow
progress to the shore.
Time's measured beat seems stalled,
the languid air
scarce able to sustain itself for heaviness.

The children, busy at their play
with an old fish-box, while contented time away
as if eternity was theirs,
to childhood's happy day no end,
blind to what woes
that cloud might yet portend.

Morning Milk

One sound
I most associate with my childhood days,
which, of a morning, would awaken me,
either to sunshine's Summer haze -
a lazy playing upon still-drawn black-out blinds -
or if in Winter time
to windows upon which Jack Frost
had set his icy braille.
To listen for it now would be to list' to no avail.

I'm thinking of the ringing clip-clop-clip
of iron-shod hooves,
beating tattoo upon
the cobblestones' hard ground,
the jingling music of the harness's brass-bound
   accoutrements,
a stately trot,
horse slowing to a stop,
the jangling clash of full or empty crates,
then off again,
clip-clop-clip-clop-clip-clop.
the Co-op's horse-drawn float upon
its misty morning round.

Winter Evening: Edinburgh

The glow is almost roseate
from that snow-filled sky.
Against it, row by row,
the tall, gaunt buildings rise
into the wintry stillness
of a fading afternoon.
The light will go quite soon
and frost begin to bite.
Shoppers in busy buses will go home
leaving to revellers of every kind -
concert, theatre, club and cinema goers,
pub crawlers and kerb walkers -
the approaching night.
Yet with the darkness comes
the gaiety of light,
shop windows brightly lit,
bold neon signs,
the gleaming tracks of the tram lines
inexorably bent upon the infinite.

Elizabethan [2]

Old oil drums, grimy with neglect
and rust encrusted, lie forgotten at the end
of the bay platform, rank as the seeded

weeds between the ordered paving slabs,
uncomfortable as a seat to sit upon
for more than many minutes

but my daily destination after school,
and little more than moments from my home
nearby.

Here I'd await whichever A4 brought
the crack Elizabethan in each day
to Waverly, the engine running light

to pass Haymarket station on its way
to Roseburn, and a stabling overnight,
enabling next day's journey back down south,

some dull old favourite the usual fare,
Merlin or Union of South Africa:
but what we hoped for was a Kings Cross based

A4, a 'cop', that we'd not seen before.
Do children do trainspotting yet?
What trains today would be worth waiting for?

Those proud pacifics have all had their day,
the oil drums too have gone the self-same way,
and tramlines run where there was once a bay.

Adagio Molto Moderato [3]

Franz Schmidt's Third Symphony,
first movement, marked
Adagio Molto Moderato, opening theme
a rising musical motif,
aspirant in character, of optimistic mood.
I hear the tune again as I first heard it,
not in orchestral guise
but as my father played it on Gran's piano,
drifting upstairs to where we children,
gone to bed, lay listening,
its rising cadences sustaining the day's sunshine,
keeping sleep at bay,
a sound that spelt content:
Adagio Molto Moderato,
moving with leisure, an unhurried pace:
how children-some at least, the lucky ones-
experience their days,
all blessed and blessing, gentle, kind,
before life comes a-questioning,
begins to build
its baffling hall of mirrors in the mind.

No Jobbing Decorator

Master craftsman, Mr. Magee,
atop a plank laid loose across two ladders,
oddly foreshortened to my infant eyes,
a fag between your lips,
is how I now remember you at work,
your painter's overalls pristine
in my mind's eye,
for paint and paper were for walls.

You were no jobbing decorator.
Old-school trained,
you cut no corners as you worked towards
that perfect final finish,
foundations laid painstakingly long since.

Our rooms were large, their ceilings high,
why I remember you the way I do,
picking out plaster cornices in Wedgwood Blue and gold,
watching you work an old
bland marble mantelpiece till it resembled real mahogany,
your wizardry with stain
converting all to rich dark flowing grain,
an education in itself.

When otherwise engaged you drove a van,
deliveries for McVities,
tended the duties of an elder at West Coates,
stood in for Santa Claus one Christmas,
maybe more:
in bed unwell I missed the party,
something nasty,
though you called in anyway,
resplendent in red coat, a matching hood
and long white beard.
I wasn't fooled, but happy to receive
the proffered gift you brought -
a puzzle monkey.

Mr. Robertson

How long, I wonder,
were you gardener at 5 Osborne?
A lifetime's distance
finds you fixture and archetype,
the definitive old man,
old Mr.Robertson my dad's habitual reference:
and there you stand
in shirt-sleeves, waistcoat, and flat cap,
wiry, a little stooped,
your 'piece' and blackened billy in one hand,
the only fit receptacle from which to take your tea,
ah'm daein fine, Mrs. Mimey, jist fine
in broad Scot's brogue.
You never got our name correct,
in this no different from the rest.
I wonder, did I request
that wooden sword you crafted with such care,
disdained as much too short,
no proper weapon for a knight to bear?
My infant lack of gratitude
was sharp enough to wound, if not the sword,
a painful memory,
your labour's love unkindly scorned
by a mere child.
would that I could undo
that thoughtless cruelty.

At Aberlady Bay

A day of heat and stillness,
thermals building with inexorable mass
within the great bowl of the bay,
high piling cumulus mustering like doom
along the blue horizon of the Firth
where land, sky, sea, melt into one.

A day of silence, too, the only sound,
save for the piping of small wading birds,
the plash of low incoming wavelets
over wide, wet sand.
You paddled languidly and posed,
as I, in love with all you were,
captured the golden moments on my film,
your bright pink pinafore a perfect foil
for the ubiquitous blue.

That must have been the day we fled
an empty Aberlady Church,
spooked by the marble effigy of long dead
Lady Wemyss,
uncanny in its realism there.

Still young and innocent
there was no place for death in our designs,
our living all to do.
Yet the most perfect day must end
and summer days seem rarer than they were
when we were young,
while still cloud builds along the not so far horizon where
all definition's lost.

Chagall At Tudeley: A Verse Sequence

In 1963 a tragic sailing accident off the South coast robbed Sir Henry and Lady D'Avigdor-Goldsmid and their younger daughter Chloe of their eldest daughter Sarah.

Marc Chagall. the internationally famous painter and stained glass artist was subsequently commissioned to design and make a memorial window to Sarah to be installed in All Saints Church, Tudeley, in Kent. This resulted in an offer by the artist to complete the glazing of the entire building.

In 1972 I became Vicar of Tudeley-cum-Capel with Five Oak Green. As a glass artist myself I admired the way Chagall had created a wonderful scheme of glazing to give expression to the hope embodied in the Christian gospel of Christ, crucified and risen.

There can be no true equivalence between the visual arts and poetry, yet just as I had attempted to do in the case of Tom Denny's Millennium window in my own church of All Saints in Yorkshire, I wanted to find a way – different in the case of the Tudeley windows – of conveying something of their profound significance. Seeing the windows through a number of different eyes proved something of a solution to this problem. And a way of telling their story

Theme

Sea-rocked, sea-cradled, deep a daughter lies,
in ocean's bosom beneath stormy skies,
dreaming a sea-blue dream until she rise.

The Artist

Tudeley, All Saints,
a small and ordinary church
serving some scattered houses, a few farms,
the sort of place that you might search
for on a map of Kent and miss:
hardly the high-profile project, this,
that you were used to, as at Assy,
the Jewish synagogue, Jerusalem,
or Metz, the most ambitious of these three
where stained and painted lights spill
colour from the apses, transept and triforium,
in tribute to your mastery and skill.

Though not acquainted with the family,
a friend in common, intermediary,
effects an introduction.
You learn of tragedy, an accident at sea,
their daughter drowned and she
but twenty one.
With some conditions you agree,
a large memorial window,
meeting a need for public as for private
recognition of their loss.

With all the poetry and pathos
of your art you will affix
the very image of her death
beneath that of the crucifix,
daring all disapproval to give breath
to grief, and grief's best hope of healing,
Love's un-reluctant gift.
And you will image all of this
with your accustomed visionary feeling.
Thus the great sweep
of glass you will deploy there,
blue as eternity,
deep as Sarah's sleep.

Critics

Your small church charms him: *I will do*
he says *the other windows too.*
Some murmur, though, thinking a Jew
quite the wrong person to fulfil
a project of this kind,
where Christian insight is required.
Could she not find
someone more suited to the task
they ask,
an honest English craftsman, tested, tried?
Yet wisdom proves you justified
and she who died
so tragically is memorialised
in glass that has inspired
many whose hearts in grief were mired
as deep as yours:
for light and colour can what words cannot,
and open doors into the human soul,
to secretly confront,
to challenge, to console.

The Agnostic

Inside the church you pause beside the door,
eyes turned to where blue light, colour of summer skies
cascades in waves upon the chancel floor
to lie in liquid heaps.
In stormy seas a girl is seen to drown, a woman weeps,
one climbs a ladder from the ocean deeps
to where Christ hangs in majesty supreme
upon the cross, and as in dream,
a mounted figure rides a crimson horse
up Calvary's way,
compounding with a sense of mystery
this scene of loss.

Here in this glass there is revealed
a tale of grief: so much is clear:
Yet how a young girl's tragic death at sea
might intersect with his,
whose arms, outstretched, embrace in agony
all pointless death and grief
is puzzle all must ponder as they will,
and go on pondering until
they answer find
or make their peace with universal ill.

The Parishioner

What did you make of it,
the wholesale transformation of your church
I mean? Some wondered then, and still.
That some ill-will
was felt would not have been surprising,
though it was not overt,
and could not be, loyalty to Sir Henry, Lady G,
and their remaining daughter
making a much conflicted thing of gratitude,
that sense of something stolen,
local and parochial, feel wrong.
Yet it persisted as an undercurrent, strong
enough to undermine relations,
cause vibrations in the long
and longer run: new altar furniture, new pews
and the east window's Gothic tracery removed,
its shape quite altered and construed
a different way.
You may have been consulted:
did you have any say?

An Incumbent

I enter quietly, take a pew,
and in imagination sit where you
were wont to do each week,
wondering that with such seeming equanimity
you could face down that glassy wall of blue
or be to Sarah's death in such proximity
as he depicted it, sequential dream
within his larger archetypal scheme
for all the world to view.

That you had turned the place into a shrine
was hard to counter, your devotion
not to be denied.
Yet once subsumed within the artist's larger notion
of a scheme, this window functions as a sign,
not of some grand design,
but of the painful journey all must take
to find some healing potion
for the pointlessness of things that make no sense,
Christ crucified a point of reference,
due deference shown to his compassionate
embrace of suffering.

Then details show their art,
the rainbow, promise of an end to suffering's smart,
the angel's chalice, drunk down to the lees,
offers reprise of life,
and near your daughter's body,
leaf in beak,
for an unfolding future, Noah's dove,
while dreaming Jacob climbs from life's long grief
to where all gain, all loss, are lit by love.

Angels

How lyrical the lead-lines are
in these two southern lights
where sunlight dances in bright swathes
of yellows, golds and whites
through layered leaves
and dim half-hinted shrubberies.
They are balletic almost,
playful, poised, and long,
artless as any line of liquid song
piped from the branches
of the one primordial tree,
by angel, or by golden-plumaged bird.
Here grief is done with,
for when peace is won,
heaven opens like the flowers half-hinted at,
and cherubs dance in step
to unheard melodies, bright metamorphoses
of things which once were denizens of night,
too shy to more than flit like fireflies
at the edge of sight.

Hymn [4]

Grieve, grieve Madonna, for your lost beloved son,
whose broken body lies in its last rigour at your feet.
Heart-fast together will Love's healing work be done,
yours not to separate the bitter from the sweet.

Bear, bear Madonna, let your gentle heart be true,
soon will Love's scattered seeds become new fruit.
Though absence pierces to the heart of you
Love's golden harvest has already taken root.

Yearn, yearn Madonna, tears of grief must ever spill,
if to a Christ-like grace you would aspire,
and Love's own shining lineaments reveal
life that is born anew in suffering's fire.

Love, love, Madonna, through your open priestly palms
Love offers yet the bread of life to Man,
Love's wine of joy in you has healing balms
which bring a wholeness nothing other can.

Live, live Madonna, live your new-made life in Him
Whose high endeavour hides such high expense:
He is your living Tree of Life, you his new limb,
Drawing from his dark roots your constant sustenance.

Pieta [5]

Beech tree,
the trunk already riven,
and with that tendency to split,
apt metaphor,
your Mater Dolorosa felt already
in the wood, waiting only for
the patient exploration
which your carver's skill might bring
to the revealing.
I wonder, did you wince much
at her woundedness,
as with such sensitivity
your tools took shavings from her cheeks,
her palms,
open as his, her son's, to suffering's imprint?
She bore her own marks of stigmata
which you added to,
gilding the wood-grain of her hood
with glint of glory,
shards of a bright mandorla yet
to be assembled.
We, whom she welcomes, reach
for her mother's touch, hungry for healing,
feeling the scald of tears,
which spill,
ruinous as rivers, from her lowered lids.

Under a Dark Sky

All day the same sad worrying wind,
subverting bright July,
sent sombre grey clouds scurrying
across an unquiet sky.

How like some sad unsettling wind
is that anxiety
from which so many suffer loss
of soul serenity.

The world's distress is all too plain,
each day ills multiply
like clouds that build, and burgeoning
crowd out a cloudless sky.

Grief soon gives birth to anger, may
find some relief in tears:
disquiet, born of nameless dread,
intensifies raw fears

sapping the soul of energy,
corroding all with doubt,
laying heart's landscape all to waste,
shutting the sunshine out.

Is there effective antidote
to pitch against such woe?
If there be one then love alone
the only one I know.

You think love too debased a word
to serve measure for measure
the ills that so beset a world
and nullify all pleasure?

You think it sentimental, trite,
to bandy such a word
within the context of the world's
complexities: absurd!

Yet only true love stays the course,
endures the darker day,
can challenge evils dark as sin
that over lives hold sway.

Use any label that you like:
by many another name
love's spirit works to bolster life:
all one and all the same.

The Forge [6]

(for Ronan)

You stand relaxed there on An Teallach's rocky tor,
a little nonchalance disguising proper pride
in your achievement, captured upon this six-by-four
by the proud father that you climbed beside.

Once, as a boy, you drew its corrie wall,
copied with care the fearsome downward plunge
of Toll an Lochain's cliffs, not yet in thrall
to woes that would your growing self estrange,

almost as if, sensing the jeopardy ahead,
you traced your own topography to come,
fathoming depths of fear and inner dread
in images your outward eyes could plumb.

Then, forging your freedom in the fire
of frailties you fought and overcame,
you hammered out upon the anvil of desire
the shape of one worthy to bear your name.

Upon An Teallach's top you can stand tall,
scanning the far horizon's blue beyond.
Here men have fallen and again may fall:
humility becomes such hard-won ground.

Parker's Piece: Winter [7]

The day has been and gone.
Frost crackles in the cold dry air.
The fading daylight of the winter afternoon
lends luminescence to a bare
naked sky from which the snow
now blanketing the wide expanse of Parker's Piece
has been swept clear.

Saint Botolph's spires climb into atmosphere
so still above the town,
the smoke that rises thinly from
the chimney pots of houses huddled down
against the chill of fenland frost
can barely rise.
Importunate leafless trees accost
the darkening skies,
reluctant to admit oncoming night.

Ice crystals wink and glitter in the light
of the one lamp that
like a frozen referee stands guard
where four ways meet.
Here on the playing fields of this seat
of learning, one hundred years ago,
Football Association Rules
found formulation in the clash of Schools,
and here, on many a summer's day,
matches of cricket might be underway,
lazy spectators ranged beneath
the tree-lined littoral of this College green.
Yet now no single soul is to be seen.
Seasons inverted,
all is now empty, bleak, deserted.

Burrell's Walk [8]

Beyond Clare Bridge,
boasting uncountable stone balls,
an avenue of limes,
new-leafed to greet the year,
consort with cherry trees,
in Spring
the ground beneath them white
with fallen blossom.
There, boldly back-lit,
bright tulips dupe the eye
into supposing blood-red poppies
blaze like flame
against the green of uncut grass,
strong dappled light
creating an impression any painter
of that school
would be a fool not to exploit.

But where the walk-way ends
in the Memorial Court,
no floral subterfuge confuses
when confronted with the dead of
two world wars,
their names, alumni of the College,
there recorded for posterity.
They too once walked this way
some idle day in Spring,
thought themselves fortunate as we
who stroll here still,
feeling the sunshine warm upon our skin.

In Anger

There are no words for this atrocity
gratuitously wrought upon Ukraine,
such wanton devastation and such pain
born of such monstrous animosity,

Putin's paranoia of the West,
nor for vile disinformation spread
so blatantly, the cruelty of lies fed
to the Russian people, which attest

to the manipulative nature of a power
which thrives, and only can, on hate and fear.
Nothing in him exists which might endear
any but those as eager at this hour

as he to challenge the democracy
and freedoms here his cronies all enjoy,
denied to most. He would destroy
all opposition to his grim autocracy

and plunge the world into the pit of hell.
Yet we are told to love our enemies,
do good to those who hate us.
Well, well, well.

Sacrificial Scena [9]

It startled me,
blundering from the bush so suddenly
it stayed my hand,
such that I dropped the sacrificial knife
whetted to such an edge
as would have spilt my son's life instantly,
the very son which was His pledge
to Sarah and to me.
What cruel inhuman test was this,
what strife,
to ask a father slay his son?
Was such the God I worshipped?
Was it not rather unbelief in me that
trusted not His word,
but yet demanded proof that He had heard
and heeded me?
Moloch had me unmanned
in that black moment's madness,
but for the ram that from the bush
blundered in sudden rush.
My heart yet hardly won,
there by the Reed Sea's strand,
I set my wondering son
to counting grains of silver sand.

A Fatuous Affair

Vituperate
as any combed and crested cockerel
with murder on its mind,
a blackbird flies in frenzy at its foe,
wings fluttering and beating in fatuity,
frantically scrabbling,
scratching with extended four-clawed feet,
but – to its consternation –
fails to drive the other one away,
bird matching blow for blow.

Baffled, it falters and falls back,
then once again goes in for the attack,
shitting in its extremity,
again, and yet again to be repulsed.
Day after day
the bird returns to the affray,
only the car's wing-mirror getting in the way
of victory,
denying either furious combatant
that last,
that final say.

Fault Lines

Violence,
ruinous as rockfall,
fractures along fault lines,
imponderable
in the way they may behave,
stable only if nothing nudges
at the indeterminate spot
where smallest pressure presages catastrophe:
as when, with one false step,
the snap of snow on a steep face
launches a white annihilation,
or sea's incursion,
at some hour not obviously different from another,
triggers a cliff's collapse.

Violence so fractures along
unsuspected lines,
injurious alike to victim and
to perpetrator both,
though differently in scale and in degree
in every case:
abuser and abused,
the bullied schoolboy, battered wife,
accuser or accused,
the highly visible and that we never see:
and fault lines run through all:
through them,
through you,
through me.

What Am I? [10]

I am a revealer,
more means than end,
invented by the Arab Alhazan,
though known to Aristotle
and the Chinese long before.
The High Renaissance masters
made an aid of me,
turned the clear logic of my seeing
through an angle
in pursuit of true perspective.
Astronomers made different use of me
in studying eclipses of the sun,
Kepler among them as you
might suppose,
while in Victorian times I was reduced
to novelty, some scientific fun
for folk intrigued
by the superior God's-eye view it gave them
of their world.
Now I am commonplace,
an adjunct to devices of all kinds,
a neutral tool,
though sinister in satellites perhaps -
spy in the sky -
or eye in the sky, drone warfare,
pin-point precision
affording untoward destruction,
darkness the end,
the closing of all eyes.

Ladyhawk [11]

Stony and steep, the track to Boscastle
edges past Western Blackapit, and there
above sea tumult, quarried gulfs of air,
our close encounter with the kestrel,

Hopkins' emblematic Christ, took place.
The bird, merely a metre from us at eye level,
hung in the vortex of the headwind, visceral
in its command and mastery of space,

with fierce intent, scanning the cliff-top verge.
Our eyes absorbed the bold heraldic colouring,
breast feathers flecked and pale, a chestnut wing,
grey hooded head, bright eye bent to the surge

of breaking waves below: no Holy Ghost,
or any ghost at all, but slipping into flight
sharp as a scimitar, scything the liquid light
that broken clouds make of a broken coast.

So might the fabled lady of the window fly,
as once her kestrel, keenly, at command
to quarter wind-bent thorn, gorse-gilded ground,
haunter and huntress in the torn fields of the sky.

A Legend for Ladyhawk [12]

There was a Cornish maiden once
who did its sea cliffs walk,
and for the Kestrel on her wrist
cat-called as 'Lady-hawk'.

She was betrothed and soon to wed
a seaman of that county,
who long aboard his ship had been
for taking the king's bounty.

Within a windy cliff-top arch
she sat at ease one morning,
and wistfully she scanned the sea
as on her kestrel fawning

she sighed: *for hope this balmy breeze*
may bring my love to me,
Till then, that you were gifted, such
that you might talk with me!

Yet now fare swiftly, fly the fields
and bring to me your kill,
for I must have some grace of game
e'er I come from this hill.

At her command the bird took flight
the moorland ground to quarter,
and sighting soon a coursing hare
stooped swiftly to the slaughter.

The hawk struck hard with fierce intent,
when, to the bird's surprise,
the hare gave piteous utterance,
as light went from its eyes.

Know you have killed your lady's love,
who coming from the sea,
met with malign misfortune in
a maid who once loved me,

for jealous of the happiness
of two who loved so well,
she sought the aid of one who cast
upon me this dread spell.

The bird returned, and speaking, told
how he her love had slain,
and how the quest to hunt and kill
had brought to her this bane.

Then was his mistress filled with rue.
Would you had never spoken,
she wept, *the tale that you have told*
has left my heart forsaken.

And I am bound this bane to share,
no more the doleful dove,
I will avenging angel be
of she who cursed our love!

Now you and I must be as one,
no more these cliff-tops walk,
and she will rue the scornful day
she dubbed me 'Lady-hawk'!

So now when on the wind is borne
a keening kestrel's cries,
one hurries homewards, fearing that
which haunts her mind's dark skies.

A Disturbing Encounter ¹³

("The other night upon the stair,
I met a man who wasn't there")

It was a rum encounter right enough,
though who or what she was we met at Minster
that September afternoon must be
a matter of conjecture.

So did we talk ourselves
into believing she was dead?
Maybe -
that said,
we were not in the aftermath
well able to explain how odd, uncanny
our encounter with her was,
for seated by the path
we should have noticed her approach,
have heard her come.
Instead,
as if she'd stepped out of thin air,
silent, unmoving, much too close,
she was just standing there,
causing a frisson, not of fear,
more of embarrassment, dismay,
as if caught trespassing
upon her space.

She was most strangely dressed
for such a place,
black city suit unsuited to the spot or day,
for those that come that way,
must come either a long walk through the wood
by steep, tree-rooted paths,
or else arrive by road.
No car was parked, nor did one pass,
that must be understood.

A Disturbing Encounter [13]

But more incongruous than her clothes
was the unseeing stare
with which she looked right through us,
almost as if we were not even there.
Then, too, the want of any word,
acknowledgement, or any greeting given,
for as we shrank to let her pass,
she glided by,
still without sound, and passed us
oh, so close, we could have touched with finger tips
her elegant coiffure,
the livid crimson of her lips,
tasted upon the air a whiff of any scent she wore.

Yet no impressions did she leave with us,
save that we saw.

Beyond us at the corner of the church,
briefly she there remained,
seeking, it seemed, someone or thing she did not find.
Was she, to our reality, quite blind?
We saw her come back to the fast shut tower door,
but though we could not say we saw her go,
saw her no more.

In all of this we'd felt no sense of dread,
no raising of the hairs upon the head,
neither of us distraught,
merely uneasy,
but left pondering the absurd,
disorientating thought:
was she alive?
Or was she -
could she have been - dead?

The Old Churchyard, Lochcarron

Erect as sentries,
upright in their indifference to grief,
save where some few
grown weary with their watching brief
lean drunkenly askew,
they stand amidst the uncut grasses
near Lochcarron shore,
aged granite guardians to the worthy
village folk of time before.

No posies grace the rose bowls,
though in eloquent confusion
of dancing yellow heads,
wild flowers bloom in profusion,
emanations of the dead,
who here, memorialised in stone,
sleep next the shore
of the sea loch, the old, the hardly grown,
the rich, the poor.

In season, flowers of every kind
and hue bloom here,
shy snowdrops
mark a start to each new year,
May's bluebell crop
preceding Summer's golden spread,
God's Summer store,
all numbered as the hairs upon each head
of those who came before.

Hillside Clachan [14]

A way winds up through birches,
climbing to open hillside
and the vestiges of long
abandoned settlement.

Here amidst tawny, bracken-
covered slopes, stony
remains of a once thriving
hillside clachan lie in heaps,

exposed to wind and weather
as, once, families to the
hardship and disease that brought
their life here to an end.

Hard to imagine now how
circumscribed their lives, cleared from
some upper glen's more hospitable
climes, must once have been:

for though the sunshine on this
February afternoon is bright,
yet Winter's chill still cloaks
the hills in white.

Autumn in Attadale

Autumn in Attadale,
where, for a while, riot of russet,
yellow, red and green
is seen in bright profusion.

Here burnished beech leaves, heaven-hung,
lie banked in glitter of gold against the waning sun,
while there, a treasure trove of leaves
lies limpid on the still dark surface of a pond
like scattered coins.

Elsewhere a feast of un-plucked berries,
dark as drying blood,
brings frolic of fieldfare
in frenzy of feathered flighting,
alighting here and there in hurried hunger,
while in the grove,
reaching from riven rock,
where clutching roots suck moisture from each crack,
the tall, gaunt conifers,
dreaming giants,
rise like spires of prayer into the ether's thin
frost hinted air,
feeling the fell of Winter nearly here.

Within the kitchen garden
Christmas Pippins bring a promise of good cheer.

Autumn Wedding [15]

(for Tracey and Keith)

A wet day for a wedding,
the October rain relentless as with
family and friends,
a favoured few,
you gathered at Courthill
to make your vows,
invoking blessing on a youthful friendship
deepened in a rediscovered love,
the stone-built chapel lit by fairy lights
and candles,
making a magic of your marriage.

Afterwards,
braving the fog-bound bends of the bealach,
it was to Applecross you went
for wine's warmth in the walled garden,
fine choice of food,
guests' tastes all catered for,
and love much multiplied in being shared.
Water there was in plentiful supply
that day, but wine,
new wine, the wine of welcome love and joy,
your brave new world,
what you will both remember.

Colour Practice: A Celebration

(for Martin & Jenny)

Sky burnished gold,
of old a symbol of the empyrean's full height,
encompasses all colours,
each one a wavelength on the spectrum of white light.
May then
your palette of a myriad rainbow days,
tinted and toned in countless daily ways -
by Sap Green hopefulness, Chinese White fears,
Rose Madder happinesses, Payne's Grey tears -
within the empyrean's gold again unite,
to mark how all the coloured times combine
to make your celebration of full fifty years more bright.

Felicitations

(for Felicity)

What should I send you after sixty years
but fond felicitations,
since neither bitter feeling nor salt tears
clouded the close of our relations?
You were quite right, you saw it could not be be,
I was too young to make you my Felicity.

There was some small disparity between our ages
not in itself important, but for this:
I was still working through my adolescent stages,
too coy to even contemplate a kiss.
Emotional maturing still to do, you found me yet
unready to play Romeo to your Juliet.

Though our attachment's tenure was but brief,
a joint infatuation I suppose,
we neither of us came to any grief
when taking the decision to foreclose.
You were not mine nor I your destiny,
we found in others our felicity.

With Small Intent

An early April day,
white cloud prevailing in a still wintry sky,
giving the lie
to an official start to Spring.

Self-isolation being the latest thing -
Covid 19,
a virus threat unseen,
decreeing it be so -

we loiter by the warm stove's rosy glow
with small intent.
People were never meant
to be thus fettered,

but the world's been bettered
by a bug
it cannot shrug
with equanimity away.

The list of dying lengthens day by day
as more fall ill,
lock-down a bitter pill
to swallow for a world that needs must work

to live and thrive. No one can shirk
the challenge of the hour
which places power
with those the world too often has denied,

the lowest paid, all those the rich deride
but build their empires on.
But when this battle's won,
will all this talk of what we're learning

alter one jot the fortunes of those yearning
for a better deal from life?
Dispel the age-old strife
between the privileged and poor?

No, it's just politicians' jaw.

Willow Warbler

I sit here in the sunshine
of an April afternoon,
lulled by the Springtime trickle
of a willow warbler's song,
a lilting cadence
melodious as water's murmur
in a mountain stream.
Above, the sky is blue,
an azure field unbroken by the trails
of passing planes.
Only a sough of softest wind,
a hum of bumblebees,
busy about blossom,
breaks the Covid-19 quiet:
that, and the fluting
of the willow warbler's song,
liquid as tears upon
the wide world's grieving cheek.

Alien Angels [16]

(Good Friday – in coronavirus lockdown)

Matthew 27.36 - "And sitting down they watched him there".

Cloaked in your PPE,
the long, blue plastic gown,
synthetic gloves,
the face-mask, cap and visor,
you muster by the bedsides,
alien angels,
armoured as any mediaeval knight
against an enemy
too small to see.
Like those you tend,
you, too, are vulnerable, anxious
and afraid,
and when your day is done,
your kit discarded
and your care put by to shape another shift,
emotions kept professionally
in check,
spill out in tears
for those you could not save,
but sat beside
to comfort, strengthen, as they died.

Praying by Number

Six weeks into the lock-down and we grow
inured to grief,
numbed by the daily numbers of the dead,
their tally told
in tens of hundreds and doled
out in doses,
inoculation, not against the virus,
but despair.

But did not Christ himself
tell us the very hairs
upon our heads were numbered too?
That not one sparrow falls
without the heavenly Father knows of it.

And when all's said and done,
numbers are merely multiples of one.
One we know how to manage, one to one,
for that's how we relate to one another,
as, it is said, the Father does to us.
There is no total sum
of grief that all must carry,
merely the grief each suffers for their own.
Give all one name, one face,
and in that one's particularity,
bring all to prayer's embrace.

Coronavirus Cuckoo

May day,
and on the hill behind the house
a covid cuckoo,
harbinger of hope, calls intermittently,
letting us know
there is no lock-down in her calendar.

Locked-down, we're going nowhere, grounded,
holidays on hold,
our blue-sky-thinking empty of vapour trails.

But with the flight already booked for her return,
necessity compels
as she pursues unsure survival for her kind,
the precious cargo of her eggs
strangely committed to an alien care,
instinctive imitation
of a faith we have abandoned, cannot share.

Is it with better hope than hers that we await
salvation of the science
our politicians daily tell us they are guided by?
The future looks uncertain for us both,
unless we change,
adapt our strategies, try what unselfish
all-too-latent love,
unheeded, calls us toward.

For there can be no competition,
instinct in all
seeking the rainbow's end,
the universal talisman
both of this crisis and its cure.
Who knows but we may yet have time enough to find
the fabled pot of gold?

Fountain

Clear water bubbles from the fountain's crown
filling the upper basin,
whence it cascades in jewelled streams and beads
into the larger bowl beneath,
a music soothing to all ears on summer days.

The bold Renaissance outline
makes a sharp, bright shape against the backdrop
of dark trees,
where birds flit to and fro, or bolder,
come to perch and drink upon its corbelled rim.

Scarlet Crocosmia, inaptly named
for Lucifer,
glows back-lit in the border, subdued fire,
while breezes stir the borders
of our bower.

Life goes about its business.
We, self-isolating from the world's contamination,
gods in our own small Eden,
sit, discontented, sipping drinks.
Clear water bubbles from the fountain's crown.

Birthing a Better World?

We always hope
but do not always think,
that this catastrophe,
the one we're living through,
will be the catalyst
to birth a better world,
that the "blitz spirit",
communal clapping of the N.H.S,
or "Breakfast's" celebratory
Half-hour-for-Heroes
will undo the world's disasters
and make all things new.
But in the aftermath,
know sadly this was not,
nor ever likely to be true.

Deluge of the Sun [17]

Listening to Rued Laanggard's symphony,
named *Deluge of the Sun*,
in late romantic idiom, though completed
just in nineteen fifty one,
       I thought
who dares do epic any more?
The drama of the soul's played out and done,
there are no places left for races to be won,
no tales of heroism spun.

Oh! To be sure, no-one can now
pull wool over our eyes,
nothing surprise a people who
have seen through everything
and think it all a sham,
don't give a damn,
save for their own small worlds.

But surely something has been lost?
When all's been tossed
upon the garbage heap what's left
but rubbish to sift through?
Perhaps, like India's poor, the classless dross
that eke a living out of doing it,
we too may find
those things we threw too eagerly away,
those bright transcendent dreams
that urged us on to build a better world.

Epiphanies like Rainbows

Epiphanies,
like rainbows,
are particular, precise,
and personal,
come unprepared for,
tend to take us unawares,
and are transformative,
creating new perspectives
and new worlds,
preclude the commonplace,
the known.

Thus, not folk-song
as a genre but
through bushes and through briars,
one folk-song in particular,
sung by an old practitioner of the art
at Ingrave,
opened Vaughan Williams' ears
to the potential of the modes.

Nor Nature
in the all-inclusive round,
but the spine-chilling sight and sound
of wild, migrating geese
found five-year-old Jim Crumley
in his Dundee home,
laying foundations for his later life
as an interpreter
of all that's wild within
his native land.

Epiphanies, like rainbows,
are precise,
particular,
quite personal
and anything but bland.

Un Pioner Extraordinaire [18]

Mont Sainte Victoire,
the mountain that he painted
time and time again,
never quite capturing
to his fastidious satisfaction
the elusive essence
that his painter's eye perceived
behind its myriad moods.

His was a promised land no pilgrimage
could take him to
save that provided by his art,
and he a Moses who descried,
but felt denied,
the substance that he sought,
a milk and honey of imagination only,
money a matter of
but small account in the great scheme
of things.

He died dissatisfied,
but to we lesser mortals was
un pioner extraordinaire
sublimely summiting where
others feared to tread,
finding no landscape loftier than
the grand abstract ideal
that he aspired to,
whether Mont Sainte Victoire,
the gloomy rocks, woods of Le Chateaux Noir,
the sun-kissed villages of Aix
or bowls of apples fetched
directly from the Garden of Hesperides,
golden or rosy, round,
and real,
    more real,
        more actual,
            more apple
than reality itself.

Peploe [19] at Prayer

What joyous colour contrasts,
vibrant patterning!
These still life paintings
gathered in one place
reveal what any one, alone, could not,
the way your favoured fabrics,
platters, jugs,
are reimagined time and time again
as if, in combination,
they possessed some secret key
to life's enigma.
Was it some ideal play in their relationships
you sought
or was it just an exploration,
as in contemplative prayer,
of that exalted state in which such things
take on the look of revelation?
As an old peasant to his priest,
I look at Him, He looks at me,
and we are happy, being we.

To Iona with Cadell [20]

Odd, now, to think another such as I,
sat here on this same hill
above the Abbey, moved by the beauty
of a place so elemental
that it seemed the Island might take flight,
each moment manifesting a persona
liquid as light's perpetual play
upon its piled array of skies and rolling waters,
its salmon-pink-white sands:
at other times
as constant as the turning of its tides,
as rooted as
its adamantine granites born of fire
when, in old time,
the gods contended for supremacy:
and still that sense of living on an edge,
where all dissolves into uncertainty
persists, and will,
while gods maintain their ancient enmity.

Cadell, who year by year
pitched up with palette, painting gear
and easel thought small beer
of those who sat within the Abbey
bowed in prayer,
bound by a God unfound:
but who's to say as much?
He, too, was looking for the light
and found it
in the Island's undeniable imperative,
its ever present flux
and lack of fixity, the quick-change God
of air, and insubstantiality.

Do all who come here to a place deemed thin,
looking for who knows what,
        hoping to see some angel enter in,
find what they came here searching for?
We are all looking for some light:
and gods, made and remade in our own image,
may for a while burn bright
until such time as, tiring of their tyrannies,
        we seek respite
in the as yet untested and untried.

And will God be ashamed of those who
seeking, did not find before they died?

Annunciation [21]

She sits unnoticed in the nave
of the cathedral,
quiet in contemplation,
or transfixed by the effulgence
of the starry rose above,
dappling the dim interior with its pattern
of kaleidoscopic light.
The spreading rays make
of her cloudy hair
an aureole echo of its greater glory.

Does she perceive there,
and with more than outward sight,
a saving grace that shapes her story?
Do the fragmented tesserae of her days
find there a path to unity?
We cannot know, and should we speculate,
may only own, as possible, what is revealed by light.
What she appears to be
may be indicative of her true state:
that halo's bright transfiguration be her happy fate.

Forest Murmurings

Seeking the sound soft Summer rain
makes falling through wet leaves,
she found, beneath low-bending boughs,
solace for lost heart's-ease.

Rain's silvery whispered sibilance,
so soothing to the ear,
brought to her troubled heart the calm
it sought in vain elsewhere.

Lulled by the forest's murmurings,
a wood-dove's sleepy song,
her heart, enchanted, quite forgot
to dwell on ancient wrong.

She wondered at the way the wind
would wake life in the trees,
and how her spirit answered to
each warmly-perfumed breeze.

Even when rains beat loudly through
the heaving canopy,
her pulse would lift and quicken to
the wild wood's symphony,

and when, in Winter, cold snows fell,
smothering bush and briar,
deep in the woodland's silent heart
hers burned with secret fire.

Spring brought shy bluebells to the glades,
white wood anemones,
murmuring birdsong, dawn and dusk,
contentment, true heart's-ease.

Beast from the East

Wind wakened me:
but only still half-conscious,
I thought myself at sea,
such was the tortured tumult of the air
beyond the bedroom walls,
gathering,
growing in successive waves,
before tumultuously breaking in a welter
round the bedroom's bows,
and if at all once seeming to recede,
only to once again renew the wild assault,
wave upon wave,
while through the boom and bust of air,
came squalls of icy rain,
drumming with mechanised intensity
upon the near capsizing boat
in which I dreamed myself adrift.

Curling my body, foetus-like,
within the warm womb of my bed
I slept again:
but in the morning woke to gale still gusting hard
and shipwreck in the garden,
where the old rowan, torn from its moorings,
lay capsized and wrecked,
its hollow heart no match for the ferocity
the wind had wrought.

Not Eunice, Dudley: Franklin perhaps.
We lost one tree,
but millions upon millions fell to winds
when three named storms
brought devastation to the land's entirety.

Deluge

Rain! Rain! Relentless rain, ruinous old rain!
Why don't you go home again, go back to Spain!
Tippling in torrents from torn, tortured skies,
trickling down your neckband, getting in your eyes,
running in rivulets down render and down roofs,
filling peoples' gumboots, imperilling horse hoofs,
rain in drainpipes and runnelling down roads,
pooling in potholes, fine for frogs and toads,
rain as loquacious as grey-haired goitred grannies,
garrulous in gutters, and gurgling in gulleys,
stiff, straight and stair-rod rain, writing-paper-ruled,
stotting off church steeples or in stairways pooled,
rain as black as blanket bogs, rain as slick as sin,
creeping under door seals, letting the damp in,
rain as sharp as sheeting, needling sad sheep,
creeping through wool fleeces, seep, seep, seep,
rain in driven droplets, dreary and depressing,
overflowing water-butts, excess rain expressing,
too much rain for motor cars, sluicing through their tyres,
too much rain for washing lines, pendent fencing wires,
beating through the branches of blackening, wet trees,
blinding weary walkers, nearly on their knees.
Where is it all coming from? Oceans, lakes and seas!
Rain as infelicity, flooding sodden fields,
rain as a calamity, beyond all average yields,
rain in cumulation, ribboning dark rocks,
rushing, roaring rivers, cutting chasms and culverts.
Rain, rain, incessant rain! Will it ever stop?
We have enough and plenty spare for those who get no drop.

Hayfields Starborough [22]:1

Lush fields of green stretch lazily away
into the stillness of a summer's day.

The early hay long since is gathered in
and distant sunshine shows corn ripening.

No likelihood of rain from that high sky of blue
threatens the hedgerows in their noontide hue.

Deep silence weighs where work's not yet to do.

Hayfields Starborough:2

Is there within this scene some distant hint
of Vincent's masterpiece *Wheatfield with Crows*?

That would indeed stretch credibility.

Yet such the threat of thunder from that sky
above green fields where, bright, the cornfield glows
some might descry equivalence, some glint
of paradox within the scene's tranquillity?

That's little sense and too much sensibility.
Persist, and where that leads, who knows?
What we have here is the epitome of high
summer, a tranquil evocation of serenity.

Yet how forlorn the fields that stretch so emptily away
devoid of life!

I see the noon-tide stillness of a summer's day,
and if an absence, that of human strife.

The darkness of the trees enclosing that bright field...
enhance the promise of its golden yield!

It seems you put on things a wholly different spin,
your eye the victim of some perverse quirk!
Because the cornfield gladdens heart and eye, and in
this scene I see no shadows lurk?

So you admit no menace in the painting even yet?
I see no smallest chance of even getting wet!

In Two Minds

When life gives rise to unforeseen
impossibilities,
things some would argue imbecilities
that can't be reconciled
with any test of sense,
and, try one's best
may not be pressed into the mould
and must at length be left behind,
discarded or declined,
wise voices say
They had to go, you know,
sooner or later:
and though you murmur *I suppose so,*
inside the *maybe* there's a *no*
since what now feels to be a cul-de-sac
once opened vistas of such plenty
nothing lack.
Best that an unrelenting Time admits
no changing of one's mind,
no wayside halt,
no way of going back.

Fuchsia

Out in the gathering darkness of
an autumn afternoon
the hanging fuchsia worries in the wind,
three chains restraining its attempt
to turn, to escape
the unquiet air's subversion.
The yellowing leaves have been set
trembling on their stalks,
a shivering agitation.
Only two pallid blooms remain
of summer's pink cascade
of tumbling flowers,
the once bright glory of the garden
stripped and bared.
Winter withers the unprepared,
prey to premonitory fears.
How quickly pass the years.

Leave-taking

You watch the clustered rowan berries
ripen on the trees,
from apricot yellow to scarlet red
turning by slow degrees,

listen to leaves on the silver birch
shiver, as if aware
of the fell approach of winter winds
that will strip the branches bare,

and lying awake in the silent hours
of a sleepless August night,
feel in your flickering pulse the last
of summer taking flight.

Sundown [23]

Beyond a wide expanse of glowing sand,
a still bright channel ebbing to the sea,
twilight already cloaks a coastal strand
backed by low hills, distant and shadowy.

The last of Summer's halcyon days is done,
the last of daylight fades from out the west
where yet the soft-edged orb of the old sun
sinks through a dusky haze to the day's rest.

A single yacht lies grounded near the flood,
a sharp edged shape against the shimmering play
of copper-coloured light from the wet mud,
moored by its crew, abandoned by the day.

Smoothed by the movement of successive tides
the glimmering mudflats glow with borrowed light.
Keel fast the dark yacht dreams and glides
through glowing metalled waters into night.

Muscle Memory [24]

If once he wept too readily
Time cured him of extravagance,
buried his grief
in deeps he could no longer find them in.
Yet still, in after-years,
tears would surprise him suddenly,
flooding dry dykes of eyes
with hot distemper,
triggered by mechanisms barely understood:
music, remembered kindnesses,
some flicker of a hope he thought long faded,
bathing his soul in momentary light,
as evening sunshine
lifts a shadowy landscape
when the last of day is done:
        almost as if
beyond his life's retreating rim,
the substance of some bright reality stood up,
        still beckoning to him.

Penny Plain R.I.P 25

Well, Penny,
you've turned up again,
returned like the proverbial coin
I never named you for,
since I could never think you bad,
more than I thought you plain,
yet looking now more like a likely lad
than that incomparable English rose
I took you for.
You can't suppose that I approve
of this new gamin look,
coquettish flair, gelled spiky hair
brushed back,
and sporting such a bold, flirtatious air?

You've come out of your shell
and no mistake,
but which the real girl,
which the fake?
Perhaps you always were the tomboy
that you now appear to inhabit with such flair!

I lay the blame quite firmly
at your new employer's door,
can but lament the mystery you were,
but are no more.

Mona Lisa Moment

Reflected and reversed
within the dark-framed Chinese mirror
Leonardo's Mona Lisa
eyes me warily, where I, ensconced within
the salmon-pink settee
remark her strangely altered image,
some sea-change.
Drained of all colour, monochromatic grey,
she's been cut out and pasted,
a Victorian scrap against a golden ground.
Peculiarly hung behind a Belfast sink
perhaps she fears that what remains of her reality
will soon be washed away
with breakfast's leftovers and crumbs,
her famous smile a little wan,
the golden butterfly adorning her grey wrist
no reassuring promise of new life.

Ways and Means

By all means seek and hope to find,
Knock at the fast shut door,
perhaps you'll find the joy you seek
but you cannot be quite sure.

For those who seek their heart's desire
may frighten off the quarry,
if too fixated on the quest
they then fall prey to worry

Best joys are all a by-product
of choosing other ends
than the pursuit of happiness,
which pays no dividends.

So if, as Alice did, you look
to meet with your Red Queen,
go where you least expect to find
her, not where she has been.

Getting it all right [26]

In railway modelling what is termed *Scalefour*
might, in religion, be what's known as Law,
a sacred path to getting all things right.

Take leave of heresy, its twisted rules
adopt our standards, use our jigs and tools,
join the society of those who've seen the light.

To call all *Scalefour* members doctrinaire,
as scribes and Pharisees, unfair.
Neither in life nor modelling is all black and white.

Perfection, though, cannot be guaranteed,
I've tried myself to follow this strict creed,
and cannot boast of anything top flight.

And though one's reach should e'er exceed one's grasp,
no door will open if too tight the hasp,
wisdom requires of all, in all, insight.

The spirit, not the letter of the Law, gives life,
unbending rigour makes for endless strife.
What may not work for one, for others might.

Habitat

Birds are particular about their habitat,
evolved to flourish,
some in woodland, or on heath,
others exploiting mudflats
or the rich resources of the sea.
Some are nocturnal,
others deploy their energy
through all the daylight hours,
but all are specialists,
and must be looked for in the places where
they are most likely to be found.

Some seem to think that God
like some rare bird
must be sought so.
Neglectful of the Dove that lives within,
they frequent places
where the 'boundaries are thin'.
Places where angels can get out and in?
Be on your guard —
— is what I say to such as these,
Perhaps God's something of a twitcher too,
and knows just how and where
                    to still find you.

Babuchka

What were you thinking of, foolish Babuchka,
pinning your hopes on a wild goose-chase,
last night refusing to go with the travellers,
this morning preparing their footsteps to trace?

Do you believe, now, the story they spun you,
kindling a flame of bright hope in your breast,
bidding you leave your safe home in the forest,
begin on a lonely, perhaps hopeless quest?

Are these the toys you long dreamt once of giving,
toys for the child that you yearned for in vain,
bright little dolls nestling one in another,
fantasy families easing your pain?

How will you find him with no star to guide you?
How far will you go, if the ways prove unkind?
*I will go on till I come to the stable
where, warm in his cradle, the star-child I'll find.*

Silent and secret Siberia's forests,
fiery and fierce be Arabia's sands,
far will you travel in search of your star-child,
through all the world's inhospitable lands.

Strangers with tales may lighten your sojourn,
jeopardy will not your purpose unbind,
setbacks and sorrows you patiently bear with,
never despairing though lagging behind.

Time will consign you to legend, Babuchka,
patron of all who come late to belief,
leaving love-tokens of joy for your children,
joy for the star-child whose joys will be brief.

What hope of finding him, no star for guiding,
how long travel on, where all ways prove unkind?
*I will go on and arrive at the stable,
and there in his cradle my star-child I'll find.*

Christmas Post [27]

Striped college scarf
wound snugly round my neck against the cold,
I walk to "Waverley" to start my shift,
the pre-dawn winter dark
foil for the festive glitter of shop windows
not yet become the focus of
the Christmas-shopping footfall of the day

In prospect, a long spell
of loading and unloading mail bags for Her Majesty
within the echoing concourse of
the station's draughty train-shed, where,
perpetual iteration of arrivals and departures
- late, or on-time, delayed -
will send me scurrying from one bleak
platform to another,
trains of intransigent caged brutes in snaking chains
in tow, loud metalled menace to
the crowds of milling travellers.

Through bleary eyes I'll watch day struggle out of bed,
make wan appearance at the platform ends,
put on some semblance of festivity
(a show of sun)
then fade and die as darkness claims the sky once more.
At four, shift finished,
I'll catch a Corporation bus to take me home: a boon.
It will be Christmas soon.

Christmas Tree

Shimmering wonder of all childhood Christmases,
flamboyant in its tinsel-rich array,
the Christmas Tree dispels dark Winter's sadnesses
in proclamation of Christ's Natal Day,

and is the mystery of God made manifest
in shining bauble and in glittering star:
its coloured candles, like the burning bush, attest
the messenger and message from afar.

By night in the bay window of the living room
a sign for every passer-by to see,
dark harbinger of joy in grief's grey tomb,
glad hub of happiness for family.

In darkness most like a luminary seeming,
its pendent branches glowing evergreen
are angel wings with needled feathers teeming,
resembling that on Sinai once seen,

for dark and light epiphanies both be
of love incarnate in the Christmas Tree.

A Bethlehem shepherd's Testimony

In after years
what he remembered
was the dance of flames
within the encroaching darkness
of the night,
cold stars, remote and bright
spangling the vault of space,
and on the further side
of the warm circle of the stable's light,
    one face
that would become in love and loss
a source of tears.

Flight into Egypt [28]

What artist's insight led you to contrive
the way light emanates from Mary's face,
which in such contrast to the wide-eyed terror
of old Joseph, straining apace
into the fear-filled dark,
carries no single trace
of the anxiety he suffers, sees no stark
weary road ahead,
but, with a child-like faith, only the way
that they must tread.
She seems not, as her husband, filled with dread
nor like the stubborn donkey,
fetched unwilling from a stable's strawy bed,
remotely stressed,
but unlike them knows all is for the best:
this, now, their test.
The child's - his candid gaze
meets ours with adult eyes -
in an occluded future lies,
which will the world she gently cradles, he protects,
   confound, amaze.

A lesser man, charged with so slight a theme,
would not have thought to make so much of it.
   You dared to dream,
exposing in your genius the jeopardy of grace
and dignity of those for whom the harsh world
   holds no place.

Nostie Christmas

On Christmas Eve,
lanterns along the path,
a twinkling star of David,
and the winter constellations
glittering like hoar frost
in the heavens.
Within, the warmth of candles,
and of hearts
touched by the love of God,
an ancient story told,
Christ's coming celebrated
in bread and wine,
another Christmas come.

Conundrum

"God is a circle whose centre is everywhere and
circumference nowhere."

St. Bonaventura

A logical impossibility?
For sure, not meant though to define,
Deity being indefinable,
but rather to confound that tendency
the left brain has to limit, fix, confine
to finite categories
what must remain ineffable,
beyond our mental grasp:

yet at the same time
hinting at confinement's opposite,
the fathomless potential of the right brain's seeing
to transcend all limitation,
feeling for God as Ground of Being
in each,
    in everything,
        in all.

Silence and Light

The climber's day is done,
his summits won.
Tired, yet content, he lingers long
upon the hill's high flanks,
caught by the way the waning summer sun
floods the glen's braes and banks,
gilding the grass heads, whin, and heather clumps.

Silence and light are one
except where from some far-off crag
an eagle's keening
sounds intermittently upon the cooling air
defining distance.

And in a moment he has flown elsewhere
on memory's wings,
five hundred miles and forty years astray,
back to a boyhood's
lambent summer evening's close of day,
standing as once he stood
awaiting trains beside a stretch of permanent way.

Silence and light are one
except where far away the approaching bark
and beat of a slow goods
flows and ebbs upon the edge of air,
defining distance.

Five hundred miles and forty years delay
the climber wakens from his reverie.
The train has passed, the bird has ceased to keen,
gone, too, the moment out of time, of simultaneity,
silence and light are one,
the silence absolute, the light serene.

Going Home

Leafing through pictures of a place
imprinted on my childhood's memory bank,
the place where I grew up in as a boy,
(in atmospheric black-and-white, of course,
Alma Mater in a 1940's Ford, a 50's fog)
I felt a longing to go back:
not to go back and live some brave new life
where all would now be changed beyond affection,
feeling, even recognition,
nor to go back and be the boy I was,
rather, quite simply to "go home",
tired of a lifetime's moving on
and the relentless march of progress,
longing for old and dear familiar things and places,
my loving parents' faces
bent down to tuck me into bed
safe and secure,
and cleansing dark to draw me
deeper than deep
into the welcoming arms
of warm, unworried,
never-ending
sleep,
the last best sinecure.

The Capture [29]

A swish of wires
and the metallic clatter of the signal arm
dropping to clear
heralds an approaching train.
Waiting turns to anticipation
and it's not long
before the rails begin to sing.

It's travelling fast,
a passenger express,
though till it bursts beneath the bridge
which blocks our view
we must contain the excitement
that the muffled rumble of approach
gives rise to.

Then, in epiphany
of lustrous Brunswick green and polished brass,
it thunders through the arch
in roiling smoke clouds, coiling steam,
the morning "Cornishman",
speeding pell-mell from Cheltenham Spa,
"Spitfire", "Sir Edward Elgar" or "Typhoon",
and past already,
Gloucester bound, then on
towards those destinations in the West
where land at last silvers to sea,
         sand,
           sun.

Bravely we wave to passing passengers
as they speed by,
hearts joined in joy of holidays begun,
till the receding rail-beats fade,
the metals cease to hum,
and we are left
breathless, bright-eyed, our senses stunned,
imaginations captured
by the sight,
      sound,
         smell,
and glory of it all,
in thrall to what will soon itself be gone:
steam's bright romance,
it's final journey done:

Life's, too, and its unguessed at brevity
when we were young.

Notes on the Poems

1. Berwick Law, a conical shaped hill of volcanic origin which stands above the East Lothian village of North Berwick.

2. A named train of the 1960's which ran non-stop between London King's Cross and Edinburgh Waverley, always hauled by a representative of Sir Nigel Gresley's A4 class streamlined Pacific locomotives, of which "Mallard" was the most famous.

3. Franz Schmidt, Austrian composer 1874-1939.

4. Written some forty years ago — in response to Fenwick Lawson's monumental "Pieta", now in Durham Cathedral — this makes for an an interesting comparison with...........................

5. A less formally liturgical, more contemplative examination of the same piece.

6. *An Teallach* – a mountain in Wester Ross, the name of which translates as the Forge.

7. A tree-lined open park belonging to Cambridge University, off which we first lived as a married couple in Harvey Road

8. A favourite Springtime walk through Cambridge's College backs.

9. Moloch — The name of a Pagan God in the Hebrew Bible associated with the practice of child sacrifice. The reference to counting grains of silver sand comes from Genesis Ch.22.v17.

10. Camera Obscura.

11. Hopkin's emblematic Christ – a reference to Gerard Manley Hopkin's poem *The Windhover*. The fabled lady of the window – the lady's window is the name of a natural stone arch on the cliffs between Boscastle and Tintagel, close to the hamlet of Trevalga. As far as I know, there is no real lady associated with this natural feature, but having invented a scenario in which she featured, and afforded her a legendary name and status I felt compelled to flesh it out, hence...

12. A legend for Ladyhawk – a fictitious attempt at creating a legend in ballad form.
13. An attempt to describe an entirely true experience outside Minster Church, Boscastle.
14. *Clachan* – The Gaelic word for a settlement or village, from clach, meaning stone.
15. *Bealach* – The Gaelic word for a high hill pass, in this case the Bealach na Ba or Pass of the cattle between Kishorn and Applecross on the West Coast. The road features some very tight hairpin bends as it ascends from sea level to 1500 feet.
16. PPE – Personal Protective Equipment: a term sadly now all too familiar to most.
17. Rued Laanggard – Danish composer and organist 1893-1952.
18. Garden of Hesperides – Greek Mythology: the Goddess Hera's garden in the west where there was either a single tree or grove of trees which produced golden apples, guarded by the daughters of Hera and Zeus. Gifts from the Gods.
19. Samuel John Peploe 1871-1935 – Scottish Colourist.
20. Francis Campbell Boileau "Bunty" Cadell: 1883-1908 – Scottish Colourist.
    The final couplet carries a double echo, one poetic and the other Biblical. The poetic echo is of Matthew Arnold's poem Thyrsis where Arnold's Thyrsis says in italics, *I wandered till I died. Roam on! The light we sought is shining still.* The Biblical echo is from the Epistle to the Hebrews Ch.11.16. *Therefore God is not ashamed to be called their God, for he has prepared for them a city. "*
21. From an unattributed photograph of the interior of Palma Cathedral.
22. David Humphrey – Hayfields near Starborough Castle, Kent – oil painting. When we had this picture restored and reframed we emailed a picture of it to my sister

who remarked that the thunderous sky suggested a storm brewing. It had always seemed to me to depict high summer, so I thought it would be fun to write a second poem by way of a *reductio ad absurdum*. This is imagined as a conversation between connoisseurs!

23   Sunset, Leigh -on-Sea – Peter Kelly – oil painting.

24. Muscle Memory- Strictly speaking the way muscles become efficient at a task by much repetition.

25. Penny Plain – the name of a no longer extant lady's fashion line, and the subject of a poem in my first book of verse *A Summoning Half Sensed*. A number of years later, the model that featured in that poem turned up looking very different in the Mona catalogue of women's clothing, My disillusion was complete!

26. Getting it all right – the motto of the Scalefour Society, the aim of which is to model railways in 4mm to the foot as accurately as possible. The Society's track and wheel standards differ markedly from those employed by the toy railway industry.

27. Brute – British Rail Universal Trolley Equipment (BRUTEs) A four wheel caged trolley with very small wheels used for moving mail bags from platform to platform, highly unmanoeuvrable when linked up together!

28. A sculptured representation of the subject in Autun Cathedral by the master mason Gislebertus.

29. The Cornishman – A famous named train of the 1960's which ran from Cheltenham Spa to Penzance. Invariably hauled by a representative of G.J.Churchward's "Castle" class 4-6-0 locomotives, to which the three named locomotives belonged.

Biographical Note

Francis Minay was born in Wigan, but grew up and received his education in Edinburgh during the 1950s and 60s. After graduating from Edinburgh College of Art, where he majored in stained glass, and gaining his certificate from Moray House Teacher Training College, he moved to Cambridge where he trained for ministry in the Church of England at Westcott House.

He served his title at Edenbridge, and after a further curacy in Bromley, took up a series of parochial appointments in Kent, Devon and finally, Yorkshire. Here he combined the pastoral care of a small rural parish with a unique chaplaincy post.

As part of the Chaplaincy to Arts & Recreation serving the Northern Dioceses of Newcastle, Durham and York, he was responsible for a number of innovative projects, including "Poems at the Palace", an exploration into spirituality through the eyes of the poets, held at the Archbishop of York's home, Bishopthorpe Palace.

In his role as Stained Glass Advisor in the Diocese of York, he oversaw a number of new commissions, and with his own Parochial Church Council commissioned the Millennium Window from the artist Tom Denny, which formed the subject of one of his poems in his previous volume *A Summoning Half Sensed*.

In retirement, he lives in the North-West Highlands of Scotland with his wife Janie, where he continues to minister to two small congregations of the Episcopal Church of Scotland. His interests are wide ranging and are reflected in both this and his previous collection of poetry.